Before You Tie the Knot

By

Maureen Witt

© 2004 by Maureen Witt. All rights reserved.

No part of this book may be reproduced, stored in a retrieval system, or transmitted by any means, electronic, mechanical, photocopying, recording, or otherwise, without written permission from the author.

ISBN: 1-4140-1423-6 (e-book)
ISBN: 1-4140-1424-4 (Paperback)

This book is printed on acid-free paper.

1stBooks – rev. 04/01/04

Acknowledgments

To Michelle Brown, M.Ed., my faithful editor and friend for which I will be forever grateful.

To Maureen Zane, my special teacher, for sharing your wisdom, encouragement and advice, thank you.

To my son Brennen for his patience every time "Mommy had to work on the book."

Prologue

I snuck into the church trying to go unnoticed. I was late. I slipped into a back pew. I could sense that the ceremony was about to start. I could see some scurrying going on in the vestibule. Whew, I did not miss it, my favorite part. Then the music, the procession began. The mother of the bride looked radiant with a touch of excitement and relief on her face. All the bridesmaids were beautiful, not a hair out of place. The cathedral ceiling was the ultimate backdrop with candelabras and pedestal floral arrangements framing the long isle. The church was relatively full and all I could think about was that this couple must be pretty special to have touched the lives of so many. "Here Comes the Bride," rang out in the background and there she was, absolutely stunning with a soft smile offering a sense of calm. I watched her as she elegantly walked closer and as she passed I caught her eye and she gave me a little wink. I knew everything would go off without a hitch, I am *so* glad I gave her a copy of my book…

The Dress

Now you are beginning the journey of planning your wedding. The first step is to decide what time of year you would like to get married. Once the date is set with the church, reception hall or alternative location, the fun begins. It is time to hunt for that perfect dress. There are several different types of bridal shops. Some are small boutiques with "one on one" service that cater to your every need. The smaller stores usually carry gowns that are exclusive to their store and carry an exclusive price tag. The "buy off-the-rack stores" have a wide variety of styles and prices but may lack in service. The larger bridal salons also carry a complete line of bridal manufacturers, where you may try on samples and then special order your gown about 6 to 9 months in advance.

Before you visit a store, start to look through bridal magazines to get an idea of the type of gown you are looking for. When you see something you like, check for store listings and make an appointment to view the dress. Most salons recommend an appointment and, if possible, try to go during a weekday so you will receive the best service. This will get you started. I recommend you try out different stores and eventually you will find the store that is right for you.

When you register at each store I highly recommend you fib about your wedding date, (trust me, this will ensure your gown and your bridesmaid gowns are in on time). Then when your order(s) arrive you can confess and tell the store the true wedding date to coordinate with fittings and the pick-up of your gown. Also, if you do not wish to be on any mailing lists, you should specify this to the store. When you are working with the bridal consultants keep in mind if at anytime you are dissatisfied with them for whatever reason, ask for a new one. It is that simple. In most cases the store will refer you to a manager or top consultant. This is a joyous time of your life, so do not let anyone spoil it. Let the consultant know your budget upfront. A good consultant can work within most any budget. Once you have narrowed down your options to a specific style, describe it to your consultant so they can try to match it with something in stock. It is best to bring any pictures with you of gowns that you are interested in and either leave them in the books or record the page number, issue month and year so the consultant can look up style numbers and price information. If you have not tried on any dresses then try on a variety of different styles (you may very well end up with the first gown you

try on). A good rule of thumb is to choose the gown that best compliments your figure. It may not end up being the latest trend you admired in the bridal books, but you will be happy in the long run when you look back at your wedding pictures. Here are a few tips based on your body type to help you when choosing your gown:

<u>Petite and short waistline</u>- princess cut gown with chapel length train

<u>Tall and thin</u>- try a dropped waist or sheath gown with cathedral length train

<u>Full figured</u>- simple lines, princess or a-line style with floor length veil

Also, pay attention to your shoulders. If you are broad shouldered you may not want to choose a gown with full sleeves.

I have heard many brides say they knew they found the right dress the moment they tried it on. Going with your first instinct has proven successful. Keep in mind that sometimes less is more. The dress may look and cost a "million bucks", but you want people to see a beautiful bride *in* a beautiful a dress. While making your final choice make sure that you talk with the alterations department to discuss any

questions or concerns about the fit of your gown or any changes you are requesting. The consultant may promise the world, but it is best to confirm everything with a seamstress and get prices in writing when quoted to you.

Please remember that bridal gowns may become discontinued at anytime, so when you find your dress I strongly suggest you order it; this goes for bridesmaid dresses and any other orderable item.

Unfortunately ordering your gown or bridesmaid dresses is similar to buying a car. You will find yourself playing the price war game with different stores. Most bridal salons will price match or beat another stores price by 10 to 15%. However, if you do not ask for a discount your consultant probably will not offer one if it looks like you are set to order. They might even try to force the sale and give you a discount with a time limit. Overall, if you are happy with the service, you have been given a fair price, and you were not pushed into your decision then you should feel confident about ordering with that specific store.

Now you are ready to order your gown. Remember to read the fine print. Most stores specify that once an order is placed with the

manufacturer there are no cancellations accepted, and the full balance will be due upon arrival of the dress. You might be told that your dress will take 4 to 6 months to come in and the balance will be due then. However, your dress could arrive early and only take two weeks if the manufacturer has one in stock and you might be expected to pay the balance right away. Make sure you fully understand the store policies.

Most stores require a 50% down payment as a deposit. Provide the store with the minimum down payment requirement and, if possible, use a credit card for your purchase. If problems do arise it is much easier to dispute a credit card purchase. Preserve all copies of receipts.

After you order your dress, ask the consultant or ordering office to notify you when your order was officially placed. **Request that the bridal shop calls you when the order confirmation was received and what they indicate the expected delivery date to be (you have the right to know).** By being this efficient, the store will stay on top of your order and ensure a smoother process for you. Remember the saying: "the squeaky wheel gets the most oil." Well, it should work in this situation, but try not to be too squeaky!

Around the same time you order your gown you should have tried on several headpieces if you are interested in wearing one. Trying a headpiece on with your gown will give you the overall effect. You do not necessarily have to order your headpiece right away. They usually take 6 to 8 weeks to come in. However, it is best not to lose focus and overlook the search for the right headpiece. I believe the headpiece should never take away from the dress or the individual. Look for something that compliments your dress and that will work with your hair type. Keep in mind that most headpiece companies offer changes (i.e., different veil lengths or veil edging and coloring). You might fall in love with a headpiece and find that the layers of veiling are hiding the back of your dress. This can be changed. If your dress is ivory, silk, diamond white or anything other then true white, you can send a swatch from your gown along with the headpiece order and the headpiece will be dyed to match. This should not be of any additional expense to you. Think about wearing a headpiece with detachable veiling. At the reception you can alter the headpiece to a less formal look.

Once the store notifies you that the gown and/or headpiece have arrived, go immediately to the store and try everything on. This is crucial for several reasons:

1) Confirm that it is the right dress and headpiece.

2) Check for the designer labels.

3) Verify the size and color.

4) Check for flaws.

This will give you a good idea about how the dress fits you, and if there is a manufacturer defect the dress might be sent back if time allows. These same rules apply for the bridesmaid order. Go into the store yourself to check the dresses and also have each bridesmaid try on their dress as well. Again, look for correct sizes and any special changes. Compare each dress to verify proper color match. It has happened in the past that some bridal salons have tried to pull off store made gowns or samples versus the gowns coming from the actual designer. Reasons for this may be that the bridal gown or bridesmaid dresses were discontinued and the store was unable to order them, or the store was on bad terms with the manufacturer and even if matters were cleared up, time may not allow the order to be

filled. Occasionally the manufacturer will have issues and cannot produce the dresses. Ideally the store should be up front with the consumer and discuss the options. However, it has been known in the past that the store might try to cover up any mistakes to save the sale, and the bride is unaware of any problems until it is too late. If something does not look right to you, ask to see the sample so you may compare your gown to it. If the sample has magically disappeared, ask to see another dress by the same designer and compare craftsmanship. If you are suspicious of something, ask to see the packing slip or invoice from your order (they can block out the store information so all you need to see is the itemized order and the date it was received). It is highly unlikely that you will have to go this far but I thought I would give you some tips in case you find yourself in that situation. Overall, allowing plenty of time will help alleviate these issues if they should arise.

Bridesmaid Dresses

It is a frustrating task trying to please everyone. You can listen to all of your bridesmaids' opinions but ultimately it is *your* wedding and it should be *your* ultimate decision. There always seems to be one in the group that will give you headaches, but try not to stress about it. If they truly care about you and your special day then they really shouldn't worry <u>too</u> much about what they're wearing. Most bridesmaids appreciate a dress that they could wear again. They want something relatively inexpensive and in a style and color that compliments their coloring and figures. I have heard this a thousand times. The good news is that this is not an impossible task. There are several off-the-rack shops to check out. If that works for you, it will save you the worry of the ordering process. Keep in mind that the designers usually come out with their new dress lines in the fall and spring so when you are shopping for spring dresses you will find new styles in the fall. If your dresses do require ordering, allow at least 6 months for the ordering process and be sure to stay on top of your order. The store will not place the order until all the bridesmaids have been measured and paid their deposits. Watch that closely. Sometimes a bridesmaid will go in, try on the dress, and leave without being

measured. Occasionally they'll decide to only put half of the deposit down. If you are not aware of this, your order may sit unnoticed.

Allow enough time for delays. Keep in mind that all dresses must be ordered together to guarantee the same dye lot. Place orders for any fabric you may need (i.e., junior bridesmaid dress, swatches, etc.) at the same time you order the dresses.

If the dresses you have chosen are floor length and you have bridesmaids over 5'6", make sure your consultant checks for adequate length of the dress. Extra length may have to be ordered. The measuring process will run similar to when you ordered your gown. If you did not order a gown, the measuring process should be explained to you at the time of the bridesmaid order.

For some reason, the measuring never seems to run smoothly with the bridesmaids. The bridal shop usually suggests a size that appears to be too big. This is not intended to be an insult. They are matching the measurements with the manufacture's size chart. The store is required to choose the largest size to ensure a proper fit. The dresses are cut in bulk and are not custom made to your body. Custom fitting

is inevitable. In the event of a pregnant bridesmaid, the seamstress will be able to determine the size and fit her accordingly. They will usually over-estimate. If someone becomes pregnant after the dresses are ordered, the dress can be gusseted (another purpose for ordering extra fabric). Another solution to this situation is adding leftover fabric from the hems to the side seams of the dress. If you have not found out already, make sure you learn the designer of your dresses. The store will usually reveal this information once deposits have been put down. This might come in handy later.

Shoes for Bridesmaids

If you can find shoes that compliment the dress and do not have to be dyed, go for it. My bridesmaids wore black velvet skirts so I had them all wear velvet shoes and choose the style they wanted. It ran smooth as silk.

If you do get involved with "dyeables" for yourself or for the bridesmaids, talk directly to the person who will be dyeing your shoes. Find out how much experience they have (this is crucial). You can even ask to see samples that they have done. I recommend having the shoes dyed at the same store you purchased them. This way if there are any errors, the store can easily replace the shoe and re-dye it. Buying shoes at one store and having them dyed at another can be problematic because there are rarely guarantees, and charges are added. Once you've obtained a comfort level within a certain store, have all of your bridesmaids try on and purchase the chosen shoes. A variation of heel heights can be an option as long as all the shoes are similar and have the same fabrication.

After your bridesmaids have purchased the shoes, have them give them to you to bring back for the dyeing process. **Make sure you label all boxes and both shoes with each person's name on them**

(either inside each shoe with pencil or a small label on the bottom). Labeling the shoes will eliminate fitting problems when they get the shoes back. One size seven shoe might be different than another, and some girls may have added pads in their shoes for comfort. Always have shoes dyed from a swatch of the actual dress and approve a swatch from the shoe dyer before they dye all the shoes. It is nearly impossible to dye a shoe, especially pastels, and have it match perfectly in daylight or indoor lighting. Indicate what type of lighting for which you want the shoes dyed.

Taupe and most light colors usually look pink in the sunlight because of the UV light. (Hint: the dyer could add yellow in the mixture to counteract the pink). Dyeing can also shrink up the shoe a half size due to the stiffening of the fabric. Make sure the shoes are tried on after they are dyed and stretched out. Using a shoe stretcher or walking around the house in the shoes and socks can achieve this. You might want to ask about waterproofing the shoes if you are having an outdoor wedding.

Oh, and P.S. "Good Luck."

Showers

Wedding Shower Tips

Bring a notebook and pen for a bridesmaid to record the gifts on a pre-printed name and address list. This will keep all information at you fingertips when writing thank you notes.

Bring a knife to cut boxes.

Bring garbage bags for wrapping paper if the facility does not supply it.

Ask the facility if centerpieces are provided or come up with a creative alternative.

Have fun with favors and have something that is usable (at my shower they gave garden tools and small potted plants).

Instead of table numbers have table names (i.e. words associated with a wedding or marriage). This idea can be continued at the reception.

Check into having a morning shower and serve brunch so your guests will have the rest of the day to themselves.

Create a theme.

Have the bridesmaids begin to prep the gifts by getting the cards open and start the gift opening during dessert.

A good alternative to a Sunday afternoon shower could be a Friday evening shower in a more relaxed atmosphere.

Play a quick game to gamble for the centerpiece. Here are a few suggestions.

Dice game: Give each table a pair of dice and have each person start rolling one at a time. Set a timer. If someone rolls doubles, then they grab the centerpiece. If someone else rolls doubles then they steal it away. When the time is up, the one with the centerpiece wins.

Wedding Bingo: Hand out blank bingo sheets and ask the guests to fill out the squares with what they think the gifts will be that the bride will open at the shower. As the gifts are opened the guests will cross off their cards and when they get BINGO they will receive a small prize. Believe me this will hold their attention.

Personal Shower Ideas

Check to see if any day spas will stay open on a Friday night and have your bridesmaids enjoy a spa night before the wedding.

Turn a Tupperware® party into a personal shower. The hostess should send out catalogs to all the guests and they could then order for the bride. The hostess can coordinate so there are not any duplicates. The bride is invited to a "Tupperware party®" and the gifts that are demonstrated are all given to the bride at the end. (She will love it).

Have a manicure party at home. All of the bridesmaids can give each other manicures and the bride could have hers done by a professional manicurist. Top the evening off with a night on the town.

Gown Fittings

Bring proper undergarments to all fittings! Include the shoes you will be wearing, your brassiere, slip or crinoline. This is crucial to the fit of your gown. Avoid make-up or lipstick because you will be at risk of staining the dress.

I also recommend you bring someone along to the fittings. Have them take notes so you will remember what was "promised" to you and what you should expect for the next fitting.

For strapless gowns, bra-cups can be used. Be aware that these are more like fillers. They do not give any support and they can be seen through most satin bodices. You might be better off wearing a long-line brassiere. Shop around for one that is comfortable (if that is possible) and keep in mind that white shows through white. Ivory is a great alternative.

Don't settle if your dress is uncomfortable in any way. Here are some tricks of the trade to help you in many circumstances.

- Sequin Gowns- Make sure all sequins are clipped out of any inseams and all areas that are in contact with your skin. Red marks all over your neck on your wedding day should not be

the aspired look. Check all seams and armholes for sequins or beads that could be irritating to the skin. A good seamstress will check this for you and possibly line the areas with a comfortable material.

- <u>V-Neck Dresses</u> – Beware of necklines that are lower than you expected due to a sample that did not fit properly. The seamstress can add lace or beading to the contour of the neckline to help this situation. In the event of a V-neck back that is too low, the same thing may be done. Have someone pay close attention to see if your brassiere shows in the back as you move around. The dress or brassiere should be altered to correct the problem.

- <u>Sheath Gowns</u>- If your gown has to be shortened considerably, make sure the slit in back is raised. You will appreciate this when you try to walk down the aisle and dance at the reception. You might not notice the problem until your second or final fitting. Also, inquire about how the seamstress plans

on hemming your gown. Most all gowns can be hemmed from the bottom even if it has a lace border. The lace <u>can</u> be removed and sewn back on for your final fitting. This is a lot of work however you should not have to pay extra since this is how 99% of the gowns are designed. I feel this is a much better way to shorten the dress then hemming the dress from the waistline. Sometimes when a dress is hemmed from the waist the dress may not lie on your body as nice as it did originally. Always bring the exact shoes you will be wearing to all fittings. If you do not have your shoes yet, then wear shoes that are the exact heel height you will be wearing. Also, if your hemline is scalloped or has dangling lace, do not get shoes that have decorative clips or beading that may catch on your dress. Make sure the dress is not too tight. Practice sitting down in the dress during the fitting to make sure it is comfortable. Keep in mind that once a dress is sewn and not just pinned, it will feel considerably tighter.

- <u>Off The Shoulder Gowns-</u>Gowns that are off the shoulder have elastic bands underneath the design to help keep the neckline in place. Make sure these are snug and comfortable. Don't forget to work on those tan lines. A smooth even color is the way to go if you are baring a little skin.

- <u>Full Gowns-</u> If you are going to be wearing a crinoline make sure you bring the **exact** one you will be wearing to all fittings. The slip can change the length of the dress considerably. Usually the slip will need to be hemmed. If you borrow one, make sure you check the length. Also, have that same someone make sure your slip does not show in the back if your gown is backless or has a low V. The slip <u>can</u> be altered so it will not show. Don't let anyone tell you otherwise.

- <u>All Gowns (including bridesmaids)-</u> Have dress shields sewn in your dress. These are little cotton ovals that are sewn in the underarm. This will absorb perspiration and also protect the

gown from deodorant stains. Bra clips are also great. These are sewn in the shoulder of the dress and you can clip your bra to them so the dress and bra will not slip. For size D cup and over, you might find that having a long-line bra sewn into the actual dress can help.

Ask the alteration department if the store plans to steam or press your gown. This should be included in the alteration cost. Make sure that they press out any inseams that were altered. Some stores just steam the gowns, which I think affects the crispness and leaves the seams bumpy. A professional steam iron is the best solution. Also have the store press and steam your veil and slip. There are some stores out there that suggest you put your slip in the dryer on cool to fluff it up. Don't stand for it. If the shop is full service, then you should get nothing less. You will probably have three fittings. I highly recommend having a final "try-on" once everything is complete.

Many of these guidelines apply to the bridesmaids' fittings as well. One very important rule is to have the tallest bridesmaid go in first, (with you if possible) and determine the hem length. Have that

noted so when the remainder of the party goes in they have the same hem, (X amount of inches from the floor with shoes). The exact hem length will enhance the overall unity of you bridal party and wedding pictures. You should make the final decision over the hem length, if not, the seamstress or bridesmaid might decide. If the bridesmaids want to seek optional seamstresses, make sure you let them know the hem height or any other changes that are going to be made to the dresses.

Final Preparations

Picking up Your Gown

Utilize a large van or station wagon if needed. Your gown will have the train extended and you will want to try and prevent wrinkling it. If someone else goes to pick up your gown or if you go yourself, have a checklist of everything you ordered or are expecting to pick-up. Chances are, unless you notify the store of your other accessories such as a headpiece or crinoline, you will be walking down the aisle without them.

Look over everything before you leave the store. Check to make sure the gown was pressed properly and the inside seams are pressed out. Look for loose beads or sequins, and check for any other requested details. If there is a problem, you are better off having it fixed right away. Look for any spots or stains. I am not trying to stress you out, but sometimes the iron or steamer can leave watermarks that will go unnoticed. What I am referring to are possible accidents that the store tried to slip past you. Sometimes it is best to leave things alone so you don't end up with a ring from the cleaner *and* a spot.

I do not recommend having the gown more then a week at your house since the temperature can affect the fabric. A humid climate will wrinkle a dress easily. A tulle dress should be hung uncovered. Be aware, however, that a lot of things like to stick to the tulle (pet hair, lint and yes, even bugs!) So I suggest if your gown is tulle or chiffon, you should try to pick up your gown a day or two before the wedding. No matter what type of gown you do have, try and hang the dress high so nothing is touching the floor. If you have a spare bed, lay the train out to prevent wrinkles and take all bags off. Remember to keep pets away!

P.S. Never leave your gown or your headpiece in a car for very long. Some dress manufacturers use glue on their dresses and most use glue on the headpieces. The heat from the car can actually melt the glue and everything could get damaged. (I have seen this happen).

Before You Tie The Knot

Bride's Emergency Kit

Makeup
Clear nail polish
Nail polish of the color you are wearing
Nail file
Mirror
Extra Earrings
Hair spray, Hair dryer and curling iron
Hair-pins
Brush and comb or hair pick
Safety pins
Sewing kit (include thread color of the bridesmaid dresses and tuxedos)
Toothbrush and dental floss
Mints
Antacid pills
Ibuprofen or other pain reliever
Bandage
Bottled water
Hand lotion
Feminine products
Deodorant
Tissue and or handkerchief
Cotton swabs
Extra nylons
Second pair of shoes (slippers)
Anti-static spray
Talcum powder
Handy wipes and club soda for quick spot removers
(Ask a bridesmaid to put your kit together).

Pre-Wedding Grooming

Do not do anything drastic before your wedding. If you have never had a facial, now is not a good time. Be careful not to get sun burnt and remember those tan lines if you are in the sun. Also, if you have never tried a tanning bed, you might want to skip that too.

If you have a manicure or pedicure, pick a color that is natural to your skin type. If you are wearing an open toe, bright pink might not be appropriate.

If you plan on having your make-up and hair done for your wedding, all I can say is have a trial run. This way your make-up artist and hairdresser can practice, and you will not have any surprises.

Speaking of practice, it is best to try on everything you will be wearing sometime before your wedding day. For example, the garter could be too tight or too loose and may need to be altered. Your earrings might irritate your ears or the clasp on the necklace could be loose.

The Big Day

The only thing you should worry about on the day of your wedding is yourself. If you are having your hair and make-up done, arrange to have them come to your house. If not, start your appointments early enough so you allow extra time for the unexpected.

Eat, Eat, Eat a good breakfast. Provide small sandwiches or snacks at your home or other location during pictures before the wedding. While some girls are being photographed, others can be eating. Drinking alcoholic beverages prior to being photographed is not recommended since you want to look your best in your pictures.

Have someone help you get dressed. Take off any jewelry or watches that you do not want on. Try putting a little baby powder under your arms for extra security. If you are wearing a full dress and a headpiece, the easiest way to get into the dress and slip to avoid messing up your hair and makeup, is to put the slip unzipped in the middle of the floor and put the dress unzipped over that. Step into both the dress and slip at the same time. Make sure your assistant locks the zipper on the slip and dress and secures any hook-and-eyes. Have someone tightly squeeze all the hooks closed if your train is

detachable. You do not want to lose your train as you walk down the aisle. Don't forget to clip bra clips if you have them. Finally, take a deep breath and just relax.

Miscellaneous Tips

Purchase a good wedding organizer/planner. Look for a planner that is informative as well as functional. Most of them have timelines and checklists, but also seek out one that has pockets to store information and business cards you collect. Make sure there is a place to write notes.

When choosing your wedding day, try and plan it around your monthly cycle so you won't have to worry about your period on your wedding day.

Ask the church if you can have your rehearsal on Thursday evening if you are having a Saturday wedding. This will leave Friday open for last minute preparations and hopefully give you some time to relax before your wedding day.

Remember that you are not alone; give a list (long or short) to your future spouse to accomplish to help alleviate some of the planning.

Stay healthy! All the planning can run you down so take care of yourself; you cannot afford to be sick for the big day.

At your reception, make sure the dinner is served on time and does not drag on. You can achieve this by asking the speech givers to toast during the first courses. Give this responsibility to someone you can count on.

Ask a friend to be the last one with you before you walk down the aisle to fluff your train and check your veil.

Choose a reception hall with a good size dance floor without any uneven ridges. Your guests will appreciate this.

Have your first dance before dinner when all eyes are on you. Then start your music/dancing immediately following the dinner. Otherwise there will be a lull in the evening and people will get tired and may leave early if you don't keep things moving. Remember you want your guests to have a great time and talk about your wedding for years to come.

Find out if any tables will have to be moved at the hall after dinner to accommodate the band or dancing. Knowing this in advance will help when you are figuring out the table seating. You can assign those tables to groups that will not mind if their tables are taken away.

Remember it is proper etiquette to feed the D.J. if you are having him play dinner music and the photographer and videographer. Do not forget to put your place cards in alphabetical order when you turn them in to the hall.

At the reception, have a good friend or family member announce the bridal party. This way they can add a more personal touch and pronounce the names correctly.

Visit a wedding at the reception hall prior to your wedding and take notice of the servers' attire. High top gym shoes might take away from the ambiance you are trying to create.

Tell your photographer that once the reception starts, you **do not** want to know they are around. **They should capture the moments not capture you!** (The same goes for the videographer).

If you choose to have a band play at your reception, consider also having a disc jockey. The DJ could provide dinner music as well as background music when the band is on break. Some reception halls offer dinner music as well.

Have the individual that you put in charge of the runner at the church tape and secure the runner to the floor on both ends to avoid anyone tripping on it.

Assign a very reliable and trustworthy person to secure cards to gifts and gather all gifts and cards. Have the gifts locked up during the reception. I know there have been numerous tuxedos returned with cards in the pockets.

That reminds me; ask one of the groomsmen to be responsible for returning the groom's tuxedo by either getting it from the hotel room or going to pick it up at the groom's home.

Ask friends or family members to keep track of any rental equipment. Request that they gather all equipment after the church and reception and return them for you.

Another very important aspect to look into is the parking availability at the reception. Find out if there will be valet available and if there is ample parking. You should not expect your guests to have to walk far.

After your wedding the best way to preserve your gown is neatly folded and wrapped in cheesecloth in an appropriate box that is lined with plastic. Seal the box to prevent moisture and store in a dry place like the top shelf of a closet. Avoid basements or attics. If you choose to hang your gown in a closet, make sure you use the inside loops provided in the dress instead of hanging it by the shoulders. This will stop the gown from stretching. Cover the dress with cheesecloth or a clean sheet and then a garment bag.

Did I forget to mention to enjoy the planning of your wedding? Yes, there are many details involved for just one day; however the memories you will create will remain with you forever.

The Best Advice Comes From Experience

The priest who married me gave this advice to me, "The wedding can not start without the bride, so relax and take your time, and enjoy every moment."

Maureen, November 1994

"My advice to all brides is to just let it go. My approach about three weeks before my wedding was to concentrate on the rest of my life and stop doing things for the wedding. Everything will fall into place. Three weeks before my wedding I told my mom that I did not want to hear one more word about my wedding. I said that July 12, 1997, was just one day. I wanted to concern myself with the days thereafter and you know what happened? My wedding turned out perfect. Save a few minutes before you leave for the church to spend with significant people. After all my bridesmaids left my house in the limo, my parents and I just sat and visited for a few minutes. It was wonderful. After all, what are a few minutes when you are about to change the rest of your life?"

Kellie, July 1997

"Don't stress out if your hem is not perfect."

Colleen, October 1988

"Your wedding should be a reflection of you, so do things because you want to and not because you are trying to impress someone. Also, when the photographer asks you to make a list of group shots you would like taken, take them seriously, make the list so you will not regret it later."

Donna, July 1993

"The bride and groom should do what they want without having to worry about pleasing someone else."

Judy, November 1967

"Eat your dinner so at midnight you are not starving and searching for food."

Kathleen, November 1997

"Have your mother-in-law plan the whole thing! Don't try to move and get married in the same month!"

Sara, September 1999

"My wedding was so long ago that the only advice I would have is get the gown you really want, not the one off the rack that your mom said you have to have. If you want Ivory, then get Ivory, not white because that is what your mom said you must get. Have as many bridesmaids as you want and do not give a care about what people think!!!!! Most importantly, enjoy your day as if you were a guest of honor. It is a day that can never be repeated, and it passes very quickly. All that planning is gone in a heartbeat and before you know it you are planning your own daughter's wedding."

Love, Mom October 1960

"On the day of your wedding do not be responsible for anything!"

Colette, December 1998

"Elope."

Jenny, January 1992

"I feel like it was only yesterday that I was a bride myself, even though it was more than 32 years ago. It wasn't until my sons were getting married that I learned a very valuable lesson. My daughters-in-law included me in the planning. As the mother of two sons I can't begin to express what a gift it was to be asked my opinion and to even be invited to join the bride and her bridesmaids to shop for her wedding gown. It's so very important to remember that the wedding day, though it focuses on the bride and groom, is a very special day for parents, too. The consideration of my daughters-in-law and their inclusion of me as they each planned for their Big Day endeared them to me forever, and I will always be grateful for the privilege of taking part."

Eileen, March 1968

"Remember to book your appointment with your hairdresser as soon as you know the date of your wedding. If you wait or assume they will be available, you could be very disappointed."

Jennifer, September 1989

"One thing I didn't do was leave enough time for the limos to pick me and the bridesmaids up from my house and then go pick up the groomsmen, so they got there about 10 minutes before the wedding and there was no one to seat guests.

Leave enough time between the wedding and reception to take all of your pictures. This way when the reception starts you don't have to worry about pictures. I felt like I was always being pulled away to take pictures with different family and friend groups, etc. It cut into the time to just enjoy my guests and my reception.

If you can't afford a wedding coordinator, think about putting a close friend in charge. It is a great way to get one more person involved in your wedding and make them feel important. This way you don't need to worry about the wedding license, gifts, the reception hall, leaving the ring bearer pillow at the church, and all

those other little things. Also he or she can introduce the bridal party at the reception since they probably know how to pronounce the names right. They will feel honored to be such a huge part of your wedding. It worked great for me."

Micki, July 1994

"Never let your parents move the day after your wedding. It is enough to give you ulcers! You have to pack the underwear you wore that night and never return to your bedroom again!"

Kellie, June 1997

"If it is out of your control do not worry about it, like the weather or other problems."

Marie, January 1969

"The day is not all about you; you may be the star, but remember your parents are the producers."

Dolores, May 1966

"Remember your vows and keep them."

Marie, August 1949

"Before you hire your band or DJ, go and listen to them at another wedding to make sure they are not too loud."

Kathleen, January 1959

"While you are sitting at the head table, take a few minutes to just look around and absorb everyone and everything because the entire day goes by so fast."

Patty, April 1991

"Do not book an early flight for your honeymoon the next day. Take a day in between to rest."

Cheryl, June 1990

"Taste test the food from the reception hall!"

Dina, February 1991

"Try and have your church and reception close together so it is more convenient for your guests, and this way more people may go to the church. Also hire a professional videographer and research them. It is worth it."

Jean, February 1998

"The day goes by very fast so cherish it!"

Darlene, October 1994

"Do not let the guys hold drinks on the dance floor during the garter toss."

Kathy, October 1986

"Have a responsible family member check you in to your hotel room the day of your wedding so your room is available when you arrive that evening. Even if you have reservations and a confirmation number, the hotel could still sell your room."

Helen, May 1969

"Go to a music fair provided by the church and actually review all the music that will be played at your ceremony."

Kathleen, November 1994

"Ask if you can sit during your wedding ceremony instead of kneeling the entire time."

Tom, February 1998

"Keep open lines of communication with your future spouse."

Rita, March 1963

"If you put as much into your marriage as you do for the planning of your wedding, you will remain happy."

Michele, June 1993

"Enjoy the day, it goes by really fast. Try not to fight with your new husband on your wedding day you will have plenty of time for that."

Wendi, June 1993

"It is your wedding not anyone else's, so do what you want to do. When picking your bridesmaids, make sure you choose friends who are helpful and are true lifelong friends. Choose the kind of friends who will be at your 25th anniversary party. Pictures are very important and capture every moment. Make sure you choose a photographer who is excellent and knows what you want and what pictures you want taken. Just because they are the most expensive does not always mean they are the best. It does not hurt to write down certain pictures you want taken and with whom. When the big day finally arrives just relax, everything will go fine. Enjoy yourself and have a good time at your reception."

Mary Jo, May 1991

"Keep a sense of Humor."

Diane, July 1963

"Something will probably go wrong but do not let it bother you. Have all your pictures taken before dinner."

Karen, August 1995

"Try and respect other feelings but since it is your wedding you should do what you ultimately want."

Kris, September 1998

After you are married, share all your experiences with future brides.

Best Wishes! *Maureen*

Wedding Planner

Timeline

Immediately Following Your Engagement

- Buy a wedding planner and memory album.

- Send engagement announcement to newspapers. (optional)

- Discuss all aspects of the wedding with your families (budget, style, size, etc.). Decide who will pay for what.

- Make out guest list so you can get an estimate, this will help when viewing reception sites.

- Meet with your clergy member to schedule wedding date and premarital counseling.

- Make lists of and discuss various ceremony and reception sites. Go to view them as soon as possible as many will book months in advance. <u>The Internet is a great tool for researching.</u>

- If it is not included with the reception site, begin looking at caterers and ask for estimates from those you are considering. Begin looking at bakers for your wedding cake and ask for estimates.

- Choose bridesmaids and groomsmen.

- Begin discussing honeymoon plans. Make a final decision as soon as possible as booking months in advance will save you money.

- Begin discussing and looking for your post-wedding home.

At Least 6 to 8 Months Before Wedding

- Reserve a block of hotel rooms for your guests traveling from out of town. Also if needed, book a room for you and your new spouse for your wedding night.

- Complete your guest list.

- Select and order a wedding gown, bridesmaid gowns and tuxedos.

- When selecting ushers, use one usher for every 40-50 guests.

- Make your final catering and reception choices and book them as soon as possible.

- Make your final honeymoon plans. Contact a travel agent to make reservations and purchase tickets.

- Choose a musician(s) for your ceremony music and reception entertainment.

- Make an appointment with a hairdresser for the bride and possibly bridesmaids.

At Least 4 to 6 Months Before Wedding

- If traveling outside the U.S. for your honeymoon, apply for your passports. These can take as long as 90 days to process. Forms can be picked up at most post offices.
- Order wedding invitations and thank you cards.
- Finalize your post-wedding living arrangements.
- Plan your rehearsal dinner (time, place, etc.). Traditionally the groom's parents host the rehearsal dinner.
- Book a limousine or other transportation to and from both the ceremony and reception.
- Contact florists and get estimates for floral arrangements for the ceremony and reception.
- Hire a Disc Jockey/M.C. for your reception.
- Consult with all companies who are providing services for your wedding. Discuss if there are any items that they may not be providing. Make arrangements to purchase these.

- Finalize choices for all bridal gown accessories (shoes, lingerie, earrings, etc.).

At Least 3 Months Before Wedding

- Mail your wedding invitations (no later then 2 months prior).
- Make sure all pertinent documents (religious, legal, medical) are completed and sent in.
- Choose wedding rings and select engravings.
- Book florist.
- Choose and purchase decorations and favors for your reception.
- Check with newspapers on their requirements for submitting wedding announcements.

At Least 2 Months Before Wedding

- Send out shower gift "thank you" cards.
- Buy a gift(s) for your spouse and gifts for members of the wedding party; don't forget the flower girl and ring bearer.
- Send wedding announcement to newspapers.

- Finalize plans for your rehearsal dinner.
- Send invitations to those who will be attending the rehearsal dinner, informing them of the exact time, place and date.
- Pick out your trousseau for wedding night and honeymoon.

At Least 1 Month Before Wedding

- Have final fitting for bridal gown and headpiece, as well as the bridesmaid's dresses.
- Confirm hotel reservations for all guests and for you and your soon to be spouse.
- Get marriage license.
- Stay current with "thank you" cards for shower gifts and early wedding presents.
- Finalize seating arrangements for the reception.

At Least 2 Weeks Before

- Prepare wedding announcements. These are to be mailed 1-2 days before the actual ceremony.

- Complete change of address cards and take them to the post office.
- Confirm all plans and details with all vendors providing services for your wedding.
- Confirm all honeymoon arrangements.
- Purchase travelers checks for the honeymoon.
- Start breaking in your wedding shoes. Wear them around the house or where you can be sure they won't get dirty.

At Least 1 Week Before

- Give a final head count, seating arrangements, and place cards to the caterer.
- Review wedding ceremony details and procedures with your wedding party.
- Pack for your honeymoon.
- Assign a trusted person to act as "troubleshooter" for all last minute problems and details. Rely on this person to help you, as you get closer to the final day.

The Day or two Before

- Give wedding rings to the Best Man.
- Place the fees for the limousine driver and the clergy into sealed envelopes. Give these to the Best Man to be handed out by him on the wedding day.
- Attend your rehearsal dinner.
- Get a great night's sleep! You've got an important day ahead of you tomorrow.

Notes

About the Author

Maureen Witt, owner and designer of Wedding Day Collections, has been in the bridal business for fifteen years as a consultant, manager and buyer. Her work with thousands of brides has made her aware of the amount of planning involved for weddings. Maureen's affiliation with the bridal business encompasses more than simply choosing the perfect gown or bridesmaid dress. Brides are constantly seeking answers regarding the preparation of their entire event. With exposure to wide varieties of ideas and resources from brides, Ms. Witt developed a strong understanding of the wedding industry. The appreciation she has received from past brides and the knowledge she attained from her experience have inspired the priceless advice shared in the publication of this book.

www.ingramcontent.com/pod-product-compliance
Ingram Content Group UK Ltd.
Pitfield, Milton Keynes, MK11 3LW, UK
UKHW041410180126
10163UKWH00012B/61